Pathways

A Journey of Healing and Rediscovery

By

Damon Heard and Deanna Heard

Pathways
First Edition 2024
Heard Multimedia
www.pathwaysbook.com
info@pathwaysbook.com
Print ISBN 979-8-9885156-8-5

eBook ISBN 979-8-98851569-2

Printed in the United States of America

Contents

FOREWORD

In the intricate tapestry of life, there are threads of joy, threads of sorrow, and threads of profound transformation. These threads intertwine, weaving a narrative of healing, growth, and resilience. This book is a testament to the power of those threads, a beacon of hope for those navigating the tumultuous waters of grief and loss.

Within these pages, you will embark on a journey of self-discovery, guided by the gentle hand of faith and the unwavering light of purpose. It is a journey marked by the profound depths of grief, the soaring heights of faith, and the transformative power of healing.

Grief is a journey unique to each individual, a labyrinth of emotions that can leave us feeling lost and alone. But within the darkness, there is also light – the light of faith, of community, and the unwavering love of a higher power. Through heartfelt stories and insightful reflections, this book illuminates the path forward, offering solace, guidance, and companionship to those who tread it.

Faith is the cornerstone of this journey, a steady anchor in the midst of life's storms. It is a source of strength, comfort, and unwavering hope. Through the lens of faith, we find meaning in the midst of suffering, purpose in the face of adversity, and redemption in the depths of despair.

But faith alone is not enough—it must be coupled with action, intention, and a willingness to embrace the journey of healing. This book is a roadmap for that journey, a guidebook for those who seek to navigate the twists and turns of grief with courage, grace, and resilience.

As you turn the pages of this book, may you find solace in its words, inspiration in its stories, and hope in its message. May it serve as a beacon of light in the darkness, a reminder that healing is possible and that joy awaits on the other side of sorrow.

Above all, may you know that you are not alone – that there are others who walk this path beside you, who share in your struggles and your triumphs, and who hold you in their hearts as you journey toward healing, wholeness, and peace.

~ **Juliet Awo**

Dedication

First, we would like to dedicate this book to God for the strength and mercy He bestowed upon us as we went through our individual Pathways that led us to each other.

Secondly, we dedicate this book to our children Damonique, Michael, Alexis, and Gideon for being our motivation during our journey. You helped give us the push we needed to move forward when, many times, we felt like falling apart.

Lastly, we dedicate this book to the memories and lives of Ramona Daneen Heard and Michael Dyrell Bookert. The untimely loss of you was the catalyst that helped birth this book. Through that tragedy, God placed a ministry in our hearts that has helped many.

Damon and DeAnna Heard

Introduction

The Journey of Rediscovery

Starts With Just a Step

"I can do all
things through him
who strengthens me."
Philippians 4:13 ESV

Laurie Jean Sennott said, "Every flower must grow through dirt." With these words in mind, we embark on a transformative journey together. Just as a flower perseveres through the challenges of the earth to blossom into something beautiful, so do we navigate life's trials and tribulations, emerging stronger and more vibrant than before. In the following chapters, we'll explore the profound depths of loss, the courageous pursuit of healing, and the exhilarating rediscovery of purpose.

This journey is not just ours; it's everyone's, a collective endeavor toward growth, love, and a renewed sense of self. As we set forth, let's remember that every step forward, no matter how small, is a testament to our strength and resilience.

A Man's Point of View:

Have you ever found yourself on a journey where every step feels like you're walking through fog, unsure of where you're headed? That's exactly how it felt for me after Mona, my rock, my partner-in-crime, passed away. Suddenly, I was a single dad trying to navigate this new world of parenting without my compass.

Mona wasn't just my wife; she was like my person for everything. We'd shoot the breeze about the most random stuff, share hilarious memes, and dish about our days. Losing her felt like losing my confidante, my best friend, my rock. We had a solid 12 years together, nearly a decade of that as a married couple. When I moved to Charlotte, she was pretty much the only friend I had (aside from the woman I moved here for initially). It's crazy how we started off as friends and ended up here. Before we got together, we were each other's go-to sounding boards for all things in life and even love.

In the blink of an eye, within just 10 days, I went from picking up some soup for her because she wasn't feeling great to her getting a positive COVID test to me becoming a widower. Life really hit me like a speeding freight train.

During that first month, I was caught up in planning memorial services and trying to figure out a new routine for my son and I. Now, let me tell you, grief was like those unpredictable waves crashing on your favorite beach. Some days, I could ride those waves, keeping my head above water. Other times, it felt like I was being pulled under, struggling to stay afloat.

A lot of those days ended with me trudging home and collapsing onto the bed. It's crazy how I used to love cooking, but I just couldn't muster up the energy to do it. The thought of cooking itself was like a punch in the gut because it reminded me so much of her – cooking was her love language, and it was a constant reminder of what I had lost.

I also became a pro at ordering food from Door Dash during that time. It was like my lifeline when I couldn't bring myself to whip up a meal. So, yeah, life was definitely coming at me fast, and I was doing my best to navigate through the chaos.

So, here I was, navigating uncharted waters, desperately craving some adult conversations. Don't get me wrong, I adore my son, but there's a limit to how deep a conversation can go with a little one. A close friend of mine suggested that I needed to find a way to connect with other adults and have those conversations without people constantly pitying me. I mean, I love my village, but their well-intentioned concern sometimes made me feel like I was on my deathbed. Mona had passed, but I was still alive and kicking.

So, what did I do? I decided to dive headfirst into the enchanting world of Facebook groups. I joined a bunch of widow/widower groups and some singles groups. Some focused on sports and various other interests. Heck, I even somehow ended up in a Dallas Cowboys group. I'm not sure if I added myself or if Mona, in one final playful act from the grave (she had quite a few in life), added me to it. But those groups became my lifeline.

They were my safe haven, where I could choose when to open up and when to keep things to myself. I wasn't ready to commit to a new relationship, but was honest about where I stood in my journey. That was my humble beginning, my way of slowly re-entering the world.

Amid all this, if I'm being completely honest, I lost my way as a Christian. Well, maybe that's not entirely accurate. I never stopped identifying as a Christian, but me and God were definitely not on the best of terms. To be frank, I didn't talk to Him for a while. For those who knew me well, that was quite a shock. I've always been a devout Christian and never hesitated to share my faith with anyone. I've even shared my testimony about my past struggles as part of a ministry to help youth, young men, and men.

Even during the eight days Mona was in the hospital, it never crossed my mind that she wouldn't make it home. I always believed her recovery would be a testament to God's love for His children and His incredible healing power. And then she passed away. And my faith took a nosedive for a while. I was more than angry. Furious might not even cover it. Add hurt, confusion, and a whole bunch of other emotions, and you'd get a glimpse into how I felt about God during that period.

One Saturday afternoon, I was lying in bed while my son was outside playing with his buddies, just like our new normal had become. And it hit me like a ton of bricks – I couldn't do this without Him. I was still harboring anger towards God. Even though deep down in my spiritual core, I knew I had to have faith in the bigger picture of why all of this was happening, my human side needed to let it all out. So, I did something I'd never done before. I yelled at God.

I told Him exactly how I felt, pouring out my pain, frustrations, and every pent-up emotion inside me.

After I'd shouted the words and let the tears flow, all I could manage to say was, "Okay, Lord, I can't do this without You. What do I need to do?" And with those 14 simple words, I reignited my relationship with Christ.

As the days turned into weeks and then months, I found myself on a path of self-discovery. Outside of God, therapy became my sanctuary, a place where I could unpack the weight of my grief and start to mend the broken pieces of my heart. It was a slow process, filled with tears, moments of clarity, and tiny victories that felt like monumental leaps forward.

Through it all, I began to see that healing wasn't about erasing the pain; it was about learning to carry it in a way that allowed me to move forward. It was about finding a new rhythm to life, one that harmonized with the melody of memories I held dear.

Then, there was this woman I met through one of those groups. We hit it off surprisingly well, and suddenly, I had someone to spend time with. At first, I thought it would just be a casual thing. I hadn't exactly had that 'ah-ha' moment in therapy yet, the one where everything starts to shift.

We saw each other for a few months, but I hadn't put in the true work on myself. I ran into a situation with this woman that caused me to completely shut down and shut her out of my life. It wasn't anything that she did. It was that I felt guilty for indulging myself with another woman when I was nowhere near close to being over my late wife. I didn't complete the work, and that caused harm to an innocent person.

It was a stark reminder that we must make sure that we are doing the work on ourselves to be prepared for when God blesses us with our future spouse. We owe it to ourselves and the person who will one day walk beside us to be whole, ready, and able to give and receive love with an open heart.

This story is about that journey. It's about the ups and downs, the moments of laughter, and the quiet reflections. It's about the road to rediscovering love and finding a way back to joy after the deepest of sorrows. Join me as I share my heart, my struggles, and my ultimate transformation. Pathways isn't just a story about falling in love again; it's a reminder that the heart has an incredible capacity for love, even after the darkest days. So, come on in, grab a seat, and let's walk this path together. Together, we'll find that love is not just something we lost but something we can find again, even in the most unexpected places.

A Woman's Point of View:

As my journey towards self-improvement and a new chapter in life began to unfold, I reflected on the pivotal moments that had shaped me. Like the moment I met Michael, and just a year after we had been dating, he asked me to marry him. I was just 20 years old, pregnant, and feeling utterly broken. What did I really know about being married? Growing up, I hadn't witnessed many examples of successful and genuinely happy marriages. Instead, I had seen unions forged out of necessity, stained by infidelity, and dissolved in divorce. As a fatherless daughter, I yearned for love and acceptance, but I lacked a true understanding of what it meant.

Looking back, I now realize that my identity could never truly be defined by marriage and motherhood alone. What I needed was a deeper connection with God, a heightened sense of self-awareness, and a lot of reflection. After 15 years of marriage, Michael had a massive heart attack, and I found myself widowed and unsure of how to pick up the pieces of my life. Doubts lingered, making me question if I was even ready to embark on the journey of self-discovery that lay ahead. I knew there was work to be done, but I had no clear roadmap. Being married for 15 years and having two children who adored their father, I recognized the magnitude of the transformation I needed to undergo in this new chapter of my life. It was time to roll up my sleeves and get to work.

Through this process, I gained a newfound clarity about my purpose, which became the driving force behind my progress. I understood that my calling lay in helping others unearth, nurture, and apply their own unique purpose in their personal, professional, and spiritual lives. Sometimes, we find ourselves in roles without a guiding hand to lead us. Personally, I had never had someone illuminate my purpose. Yet, this pursuit brought me joy untethered to material gains and a smile that radiated genuine fulfillment.

Embracing my identity in Christ and embracing my mission to support others has made navigating life's twists and turns far more manageable, even in the face of adversity. It's a journey I'm grateful to be on, one that constantly reminds me of the boundless potential within each of us to grow, learn, and thrive.

Understanding my identity in Christ and recognizing my purpose has been the rock-solid foundation that has carried me through life's toughest challenges. It's what prompted me to establish my company, with the sole aim of guiding others through their own obstacles and adversities and helping them discover and live out their purpose in every facet of life.

In the face of my own trials, I made a conscious choice not to surrender to fear or self-pity. Instead, I embraced strength and growth. This newfound resilience didn't just shape my present; it laid a crucial groundwork for my future role as a wife once more.

My faith became the cornerstone upon which I navigated this transformative period. It's incredible how our struggles can be the building blocks for tomorrow's triumphs. In the midst of my battle with depression, I grappled with overwhelming loneliness and despair, discovering the true power of placing my trust in God, even when my emotions seemed beyond words.

Now, with years of experience behind me, I find myself confronting similar emotions but with a heightened wisdom and an even deeper faith in God. This journey has shown me that faith isn't about having all the answers; it's about trusting in the process, knowing that even in the darkest moments, there's a glimmer of hope waiting to illuminate the way forward.

As we embark on this journey, there's one thing I want you to know: we're not alone. Life has its fair share of challenges, but it also brims with opportunities for growth, love, and purpose. We've traveled through stories of loss, rediscovery, and transformation, and now we stand on the brink of a new chapter.

With the foundation of faith and purpose, we are poised to take the next step forward, one that leads us to the fulfillment of our potential. We'll start at step one in chapter one by finding comfort in creating a new normal. Together, we'll explore the power of resilience and discover that our past doesn't define our future.

The road ahead is both exciting and unpredictable, but we are equipped with the tools we need, and we'll face it with unwavering courage. As we turn the pages of our lives, let's embrace the uncertainty, celebrate the victories, and learn from every twist and turn. For we're all in this together, supporting and inspiring one another.

So, are you ready? Let's dive into the chapters that await, where each moment brings us closer to a life filled with love, purpose, and the joy of rediscovery. Our journey begins now.

Chapter One

Creating a New Normal

A Woman's Point of View

God and my future were waiting on me to begin the work. "For I am about to do something new. See, I have already begun! Do you not see it? I will make a pathway through the wilderness. I will create rivers in the dry wasteland." - Isaiah 43:19

"Something new," "change," "something different" – these phrases often send ripples of discomfort through our lives. We've been navigating through life, set in our ways, following routines, and living by familiar patterns. And now, here we stand at the precipice of transformation. For many of us, this transition is both necessary and challenging.

As we delved into the complex journey of widows seeking love again, we quickly realized that some aspects of our lives needed change. We needed to begin the work. It's easy to utter words of trust in God, believing that He will provide and pave the way. However, we soon understood that God's plan also involves our active participation. James 2:26 reminds us that faith without works is dead. Even in our pursuit of love's rekindling, we came to acknowledge that there was work we needed to undertake personally. We couldn't simply speak our desires or dreams into existence; we had to roll up our sleeves and be active participants in the process.

When you've been living life according to a certain routine, a set of habits, or a pattern that doesn't yield the results you yearn for, it's a telltale sign that it's time for a change. Change, though seldom easy and rarely comfortable, is often an essential ingredient in the recipe for growth and renewal. It's not about abandoning the past; it's about evolving into the future, embracing a new normal that better aligns with our aspirations and desires. In this chapter, we'll explore the fundamental shifts we had to make and the habits we needed to establish as we embarked on our journeys of self-discovery, personal growth, and the pursuit of love once more. We'll dive into the nitty-gritty of what it takes to create new normals and set new habits that will serve as guiding lights on our path of transformation.

In the wake of acknowledging the need for change after the loss of a spouse, the journey towards establishing a new normal begins. This transition entails cultivating fresh habits, a task that can prove challenging when accustomed to a particular way of life for an extended period. Conventional wisdom suggests that it takes approximately 21 days to solidify a new habit, underscoring the fact that this transformation is a gradual process, not a quick fix. Patience, perseverance, and consistency are the cornerstones of this endeavor.

Undoubtedly, instigating change in one's life can be a discomforting experience. Barriers may arise, potentially causing delays and sparking moments of self-doubt. In those moments, the prospect of transformation might seem distant and uncertain. It's crucial to acknowledge that the path to establishing new habits is not without its obstacles.

Setting forth on a new chapter after the loss of a spouse is a courageous act infused with resilience and hope. It's a journey that necessitates self-compassion and an acknowledgment of one's inherent strength. Commencing with accepting the grieving process, allowing room for healing, and gradually envisioning a future lays the foundation for progress. Establishing realistic and attainable goals becomes a guiding light in this expedition.

These goals, whether they pertain to personal growth or professional aspirations, serve as stepping stones toward rediscovering purpose and constructing a life imbued with significance. Through this transformative process, one learns to honor the memory of the one they lost while also embracing the potential for new experiences and connections that await. It's a testament to the enduring capacity of the human spirit for renewal and growth, illustrating that even in the face of loss, the ability to forge a fulfilling future remains resolute.

Unearthing The Roots

It's human nature to react swiftly when faced with a problem or challenging situation, whether in our personal lives, families, or work. Upon discovering an issue, our instinct is to immediately seek solutions, often expending considerable time and effort in the process. Yet, in our haste to fix the problem, we may inadvertently overlook its underlying cause. Delving into the root of a problem is crucial, as it empowers us to proactively prevent its recurrence.

Consider a gardener tending to their plot of flowers or vegetables. Rather than merely trimming the surface weeds, the gardener painstakingly uproots them, ensuring they won't resurface. This metaphor holds true for effecting change in our own lives. We must identify and address the deep-seated issues that have hindered our progress.

Take, for instance, the excuses that have impeded our forward momentum. It's imperative to excavate the reasons behind our tendency to make excuses. Is it rooted in fear or perhaps a lack of confidence in our own abilities? In our shared discussions about our upbringing, we uncovered a common thread: both of us were raised by single mothers, leading to a shared absence of a father figure's validation during our formative years. This revelation prompted us to recognize the roots that needed to be unearthed.

Childhood trauma and unresolved pain can persist into adulthood, influencing our behavior and reactions. Addressing these deep-seated issues is essential for meaningful, lasting change. Who among us desires to spend their lives reacting to rejection, nursing bitterness, or nursing constant offense? Taking a proactive stance and confronting the root causes of our challenges is a formidable step toward personal growth and transformation. It's a testament to the power of introspection and a willingness to confront the past in order to forge a brighter future.

Harness The Power of The Word

Hebrews 12:15 imparts a profound truth: "Looking diligently lest any man fail of the grace of God; lest any root of bitterness springing up trouble you, and thereby many be defiled." This verse serves as a poignant reminder that bitterness if left unaddressed, can resurface and hinder our progress. It's a stark warning that when we neglect to confront the underlying issues, they will persist, thwarting our attempts at change.

Indeed, initiating change demands a concerted effort, but we can begin to forge new habits with a proactive approach. To embark on this journey, we must set practical, attainable goals and harness the full power and authority bestowed upon us by God. In the genesis of creation, God spoke the world into existence with the command, "Let there be." In that moment, He created mankind in His own image and likeness, bequeathing us with a divine inheritance of power and authority.

God eagerly awaits our active participation in the transformative process. Even in moments of doubt, when change seems elusive, it is imperative to be mindful of our declarations. If we possess the authority to decree, "Let there be," then what are we choosing to say? Are we affirming our belief in possibility or succumbing to doubt and defeatism? Our words possess the potential to shape our reality.

Embracing this truth, I began to speak of "my husband" long before our paths crossed. Even during challenging relationships, when I knew those individuals were not my destined partners, I spoke into existence the qualities I desired in my future spouse. I declared my belief in a remarkable man of God who would be my companion in life, and I held onto that belief. This shift in mindset marked the beginning of a new normal in my approach to dating, relationships, and envisioning my future.

Yet, before this transformation could take root, I had to confront and uproot the old, choking vines of my past. It was a necessary step in clearing the way for a new, flourishing chapter of my life.

Just as God spoke creation into being at the dawn of time, He has endowed us with the same transformative power through our words. Proverbs 14:10 reinforces the idea that the heart intimately knows its own bitterness. We must actively engage in the process to usher in change and cultivate new habits. It necessitates a proactive stance in addressing the root issues that influence our lives.

God has entrusted us with both power and authority; it is incumbent upon us to activate them and commence the work. This begins with vocalizing the change we desire to see in our lives and setting tangible goals to achieve it. The potency of words cannot be underestimated. Whether spoken with negativity or positivity, they carry the capacity to either tear down or build up.

Recognizing this, I resolved to infuse life into my own narrative. I embarked on a journey to establish a new normal centered around believing in the power of my words. This meant exercising caution in what I chose to say about various situations. It demanded faith – faith to trust that if I spoke it, believed it, and placed my trust in God, change was not only possible but attainable.

The Bible imparts the wisdom that "faith without works is dead." Thus, we must be willing to put in the effort and take action. A dynamic interplay between faith and action propels us toward meaningful transformation, creating a brighter, more fulfilling future.

Embrace Your New Beginning

Initiating change often entails a fresh start, particularly after losing a spouse or ending a significant relationship. Such experiences can challenge our sense of identity and self-worth. Having married at the tender age of 20 and becoming a mother to two by 23, losing my husband at 35 left me at a crossroads. My life had revolved around the roles of wife and mother for the past 15 years, and suddenly, I found myself navigating the path of single motherhood. The questions echoed in my mind: Who am I? What do I do now?

The familiar roles of adulthood as a devoted mother and partner had shifted, leaving me in a state of uncertainty. It was a pivotal moment for me to embark on a journey of self-discovery and reinvention. It's remarkably easy to lose oneself in the responsibilities of relationships and parenting. What I came to understand during this transitional phase was that I mattered. It was time to embrace change, forge new habits, and rekindle my own sense of identity and purpose. This endeavor was not without its challenges, but first and foremost, I had to acknowledge that change was not only necessary but vital.

You might be wondering, "How can I start over?" It's natural to hear advice like "put it all in God's hands" or "He will provide for you," but navigating this process after your world has been shattered can feel daunting. Even if you haven't experienced the same loss, we've all faced moments of grief and heartache – the departure of a confidant, a friend, a family member, or a cherished individual in our lives. Such losses can cast a shadow of doubt on the prospect of finding love again. Embarking on the journey of change requires concrete steps to set the process in motion:

1)Proactively Acknowledge Past Hurt and Pain:

Confronting our past wounds is the first step towards healing and growth. Acknowledging the pain allows us to begin the process of moving forward.

2)Address the Root of Our Problems:

We must identify and tackle the underlying issues holding us back from achieving lasting change. This requires a proactive approach to create a solid foundation for transformation.

3)Embrace the Power and Authority Granted by God:

Recognize the divine gift of power and authority that God has bestowed upon us. Through our words, we have the ability to speak life into our circumstances and shape our reality.

Initiate the Work of Activating Change:

Taking action is crucial. Begin the work of making intentional changes in your life, even if it starts with small steps. Progress is achieved through consistent effort.

Remember the wisdom shared in Zechariah 4:10 (NLT), "Do not despise these small beginnings, for the LORD rejoices to see the work begin...". Every small step forward is a victory in itself. While the larger picture may seem overwhelming, focusing on achievable milestones will provide encouragement and momentum toward greater triumphs. It all starts with making the decision to begin.

Initiating change is akin to embarking on a journey, one that unfolds over time rather than occurring in the blink of an eye. This expedition demands a wealth of patience, self-compassion, and an unwavering commitment to press forward, even when progress appears to be moving at a steady, deliberate pace. It's imperative to recognize that the process of change is an evolving narrative, not an immediate overhaul.

In the face of daunting circumstances or a world that may seem shattered, maintaining a positive outlook becomes the cornerstone of your endeavor. It's during these moments of uncertainty that the strength of your resolve is put to the test. It's a reminder that progress may not always be linear, and setbacks are an inevitable part of the process. Yet, in those moments of struggle and adversity, it's vital to remind yourself that you are on a path of growth and transformation. Every step, no matter how small, is a testament to your courage and determination.

Chapter Activity:

As you embark on this transformative journey, consider the following:

Focus Area for Transformation:

Reflect deeply on the area of your life that you're eager to change. Whether it pertains to personal growth, relationships, or a specific habit, this focal point will be the nucleus of your transformative journey.

Crafting Your Action Plan:

Develop a comprehensive and actionable plan to guide you toward your desired goal.

Break it down into manageable steps, setting achievable milestones along the way. This detailed roadmap will serve as your compass, offering direction and motivation during moments of doubt or uncertainty.

Remember, the journey towards change is a testament to your resilience and strength. Embrace the process, knowing that each step forward, no matter how small, is a significant stride toward your ultimate destination. Uphold a positive mindset, and stay committed to your aspirations. In doing so, you will bear witness to the transformative power of your efforts, ultimately crafting a new reality that aligns with your deepest desires and aspirations.

Notes

Chapter Two

Who are you really?

A Man's Point of View

"Honestly, I just wasn't ready," Proverbs 18:22 begins with a profound truth - that finding a treasure in life is a moment of divine favor. Whether it's your future spouse or a significant life change, this treasure holds immense value and should be cherished, protected, and shared with the world. But have you ever paused to consider if you're truly prepared to embrace such a treasure? Have you examined the readiness of your finances, career, emotions, and spiritual life? Beyond merely proclaiming your readiness, this chapter explores the importance of self-awareness and purpose in understanding where you are and where you need to go in your journey with Christ.

Imagine stumbling upon a treasure of great worth, a hidden gem you're eager to safeguard and share with the world. Perhaps it has been meticulously prepared and matured, and its value steadily increases. The process might have entailed polishing away old residue and layers of its past, revealing its true brilliance. In the same way, God's word tells us that when a man finds a wife, he finds a treasure and receives divine favor. But as the saying goes, for the woman, the question is, "Are you ready to be found?" And for the man, "Are you prepared to discover your treasure?"

Maybe it's not a lifelong commitment you seek but rather a transformative change in your life's course. Are you truly prepared for it? This is where self-awareness plays a pivotal role in shaping your future. Honesty about your current state of readiness is a fundamental step in achieving authentic personal growth. It takes courage to confront the reality of your situation and acknowledge what your circumstances genuinely look like. Recognizing when you are unprepared is the first crucial step in building a solid foundation for genuine readiness.

As we yearn for marriage, a stable home, or significant life changes, we must ask ourselves whether we can responsibly manage what we already possess. This honesty paves the way for a more authentic and effective journey toward change. Whether you're seeking personal transformation, spiritual enlightenment, or emotional well-being, this candid acknowledgment is the key to unlocking the door to your true potential.

While it may seem frustrating, the waiting season offers us a unique opportunity to delve deep into self-discovery. It provides the space for self-reflection, enabling us to honestly assess our readiness for the challenges that lie ahead. Admitting that we're not fully prepared is not a sign of weakness but a declaration of courage and wisdom. Embracing this honesty ultimately sets the stage for a more meaningful and sustainable path toward personal development and growth.

In the land of the living, God has abundant goodness in store for each of us, but it is up to us to be self-aware, acknowledge our current state of readiness, and prepare ourselves for the treasures and blessings that await us on our journey in Christ (Psalms 27:13). This chapter encourages you to embark on a journey of self-discovery, enabling you to become the person you need to be in order to embrace the treasures that life has in store for you.

Finding the Treasure in Your Relationships

Proverbs 18:22, as beautifully expressed in the New Living Translation, reveals a profound truth: "The man who finds a wife finds a treasure, and he receives favor from the Lord." But what does this mean for us as we step into new seasons of relationships and seek a life spouse? It implores us to recognize and appreciate each person's intrinsic value in our lives.

Our perspective of marriage may often be colored by superficial notions - the allure of physical attraction, the flutter of butterflies in our stomachs, and other fleeting sensations. Yet, if we consider the nature of treasures, we find that many are hidden away, buried beneath the surface, requiring diligent effort and a deep commitment to unearth. This parallels the journey of seeking a spouse or making significant life changes. It demands a willingness to delve beneath the surface, to search and invest ourselves wholeheartedly.

When seeking a spouse, it is paramount to direct our focus toward attributes that genuinely enrich our lives. This goes beyond mere physical connection, as it entails a genuine exploration of the core of a person. It involves understanding their values, aspirations, and the unique qualities that make them who they are. In this process, we unearth the treasures that lie within.

Discovering these treasures grants us insight into whether they align with our own needs and aspirations. What one person treasures may not necessarily be the perfect fit for enriching and adding value to our lives - and that's perfectly acceptable. It is a realization that each individual possesses a distinct treasure, one that may or may not resonate with our own journey.

Ultimately, the journey of unearthing treasures in relationships is a quest for authenticity and mutual enrichment. It calls for a deep commitment to understanding and appreciating the value that each person brings into our lives. In doing so, we embark on a transformative journey that leads us toward a deeper, more meaningful connection with others and, ultimately, toward a more fulfilling and purposeful life.

In this pursuit, it is equally crucial to actively seek out and embrace our own treasures. When recognized and cherished, this unique gem has the potential to profoundly enhance and enrich our lives. It may be a shared dream, a common purpose, or a profound connection that forms the bedrock of a thriving relationship.

Embracing our treasure is essential in this time of waiting. This involves a profound self-evaluation that goes beyond surface-level preferences like appearances. It's about understanding your genuine needs and desires in a spouse. While getting to know someone new, you'll assess whether they possess the qualities that align with your vision of an ideal partner. Simultaneously, as you grasp the essence of your own treasure, you'll work on nurturing and highlighting its brilliance.

Shining your Treasure

"Shining your treasure" is not merely a superficial act but a process deeply rooted in honesty and self-awareness. Being self-aware involves the ability to examine oneself critically and discern what aspects are worth preserving and which should be relinquished. It's about providing a rationale for these decisions, exercising caution, and retaining only that which genuinely serves your personal growth. This discernment enriches the process of "shining your treasure" for the benefit of your future spouse.

Consider the story of Boaz and Ruth, a beautiful illustration of divine providence and preparation. Ruth wasn't actively seeking Boaz; instead, he discovered her while she was diligently tilling the land. Her focus, preparation, and willingness to serve during her waiting period made her shine brightly, attracting the attention of a nobleman. This serves as a testament to the power of being spiritually grounded and prepared.

In our contemporary society, the prevailing attitude often leans towards acting on "when it feels right." However, this approach is inherently flawed, as it tends to prioritize emotions rooted in the material realm over the spiritual. When selecting and forming a deep connection with your future spouse, it is crucial to anchor this process in the spiritual realm.

Frequently, this journey entails a period of patient waiting. In the interludes between life's significant milestones, these stretches of waiting may appear idle, but they carry tremendous potential for personal growth. These moments offer opportunities for self-reflection and self-improvement. By setting specific and achievable objectives, you establish a guiding force that imparts direction and meaning to your journey. This deliberate approach lays the foundation for a future that is not passively endured but actively molded through spiritual growth and development.

Setting The Foundation For a Fulfilling Relationship

The effort put into self-improvement lays a solid foundation for future partnership readiness. It showcases a sincere dedication to personal growth, both independently and within the context of a relationship. The clarity of purpose, newfound knowledge, and commitment to well-being not only enhance individual lives but also form the cornerstone of a robust, balanced, and gratifying partnership.

Reflection and journaling act as gateways to self-discovery and growth. They provide a platform for processing thoughts and emotions, thereby deepening self-awareness. This heightened self-awareness, cultivated during the waiting period, becomes the cornerstone of emotional intelligence—a crucial element in establishing and nurturing a profound, meaningful connection with a future spouse.

Meaningful relationships are not limited to self; they extend to others. Family, friends, and mentors offer invaluable support, diverse perspectives, and a sense of belonging. Nurturing these connections not only enriches individual lives but also hones vital skills for constructing and sustaining a loving, respectful marriage.

Engaging in creative pursuits and pursuing passions not only brings joy but also showcases depth of character and interests. These activities serve as bridges to shared experiences, which form the heart of any enduring relationship. They foster a sense of togetherness and mutual growth that becomes the bedrock of a deeply fulfilling marriage.

By actively participating in these practices, individuals not only enhance their own lives but also establish the groundwork for a future relationship. The heightened self-awareness, refined communication skills, and capacity for shared experiences are essential components of a thriving relationship. As the waiting period draws to a close, the individual emerges not only as a more polished version of themselves but also as someone genuinely prepared to embark on a journey of love, companionship, and mutual growth with a future spouse.

When we dive into the story of Ruth and Boaz, it's like discovering a treasure of wisdom for anyone on the journey to meaningful connections. Picture this: Ruth, a woman of unwavering loyalty, standing by Naomi's side through thick and thin. She didn't shy away from hard work in the fields, showcasing her admirable qualities. Little did she know, this dedication would lead her to a fateful encounter with Boaz, a man who would forever alter the course of her life.

Their story whispers a profound truth about timing and destiny. Ruth's meeting with Boaz wasn't a mere stroke of luck but a beautiful orchestration of preparation and faith. It's a reminder that extraordinary encounters await when we trust in the journey and stay true to ourselves.

Boaz, too, is a beacon of recognizing genuine character. He saw beyond societal norms and external appearances, valuing Ruth for the remarkable person she was. Their connection is a testament to the power of mutual respect and honor in relationships. Boaz's kindness, protection, and provision are the kind of gestures that go far beyond fleeting attraction. They speak of a love grounded in a deep care for each other's well-being and dignity.

Their relationship is like a sturdy bridge built on trust, respect, and shared faith. It teaches us that true love finds its roots in a profound and lasting connection. Let's carry these lessons with us as we weave our own stories - the importance of integrity, the power of faith and preparation, and the beauty of mutual respect. They're the threads that can make our own love stories just as remarkable.

Realizing honest self-awareness

Now, let's talk about honest self-awareness - it's like tending to the soil before planting a garden. It's a crucial step in preparing ourselves for a relationship that's not just fulfilling but truly meaningful. This process calls for a willingness to dive deep into our own emotions, fears, and insecurities, armed with a healthy dose of candid introspection. It starts with embracing our vulnerabilities and understanding that it's through this raw honesty that true growth can flourish.

It means bravely facing any lingering emotional baggage from the past and recognizing how it might influence our present. By acknowledging these wounds and triggers, we pave the way for healing, ensuring we don't inadvertently carry unresolved issues into a potential relationship. This journey of self-discovery is like clearing the path for a garden to bloom, setting the stage for a relationship that can truly flourish.

Moving forward, facing our fears and insecurities plays a pivotal role in gauging our readiness for a relationship. It calls for a candid conversation with oneself, exploring what truly makes us feel vulnerable or hesitant about diving into a relationship. This might involve confronting fears of rejection, abandonment, or even the unease of baring our souls. It's about acknowledging that these feelings are perfectly normal and deserving of space and compassion to process. Often, this process calls for seeking support from trusted friends or professional guidance to gain valuable insights and effective tools for handling these emotions in a healthy and constructive manner.

Moreover, honest self-awareness extends to evaluating our own expectations and desires within a relationship. It demands that we distinguish between our authentic personal needs and external or societal pressures. This reflective process leads to a clearer grasp of our values, communication styles, and life aspirations that hold genuine significance to us. Through this, we can approach a potential relationship with a solid sense of self, recognizing the strengths we bring to the table and the reciprocity we hope to find.

In the grand scheme of things, true self-awareness is an ongoing voyage, not a final destination. It calls for a commitment to continuous introspection and a readiness to confront uncomfortable truths. Engaging in this process allows us to genuinely gauge our readiness for a relationship. This ensures that we approach potential relationships with an open heart and a genuine comprehension of our own needs and boundaries. This bedrock of self-awareness lays the foundation for a relationship built on transparency, mutual respect, and shared growth.

Living in God's Timing

Aligning our desires and timing with God's plan when seeking a spouse is pivotal, as it acknowledges a wisdom beyond our own limited perspective. Recognizing that God has a unique plan for each individual allows us to surrender our agendas and timelines, trusting that His plan is ultimately for our highest good. By doing so, we open ourselves to the possibility of a relationship that is divinely orchestrated - one that aligns with our truest selves and nurtures our spiritual growth.

Learning to trust in God's timing is a journey of faith and surrender. It means letting go of the need for immediate gratification and embracing the belief that God's timing is always perfect. This trust is nurtured through prayer, meditation, and seeking spiritual guidance. It also calls for a willingness to release control and have faith that God's plan is unfolding, even when it may not be clear in the present moment. Trusting in God's timing also means understanding that delays or apparent detours are not denials but rather opportunities for growth, refinement, and preparation for the right relationship.

Moreover, cultivating patience is essential in learning to trust God's timing. It involves recognizing that waiting is not synonymous with stagnation but rather a period of growth and self-discovery. During this time, individuals can focus on personal development, deepen their relationship with God, and refine qualities that will contribute to a healthy and harmonious relationship when the time is right.

Ultimately, aligning our desires and timing with God's plan and trusting in His timing allows us to surrender our limited perspective in favor of a higher, all-knowing wisdom. It leads to a sense of peace, contentment, and a profound belief that the right person will come into our lives at precisely the right moment, according to God's divine plan. This trust deepens our faith and acknowledges that God's timing is always in our favor, guiding us toward a relationship that not only aligns with His will but also serves our highest spiritual good.

Why must you do the self-work?

Entering a relationship without having done the necessary self-work can lead to various potential consequences. Firstly, unresolved personal issues and emotional baggage can seep into the relationship dynamic, creating strain for both individuals. This can manifest as breakdowns in communication, frequent conflicts, and an overall lack of emotional intimacy. Additionally, without a solid foundation of self-awareness and emotional maturity, individuals may struggle to navigate challenges in a healthy and constructive manner. Instead, they may resort to defensive or avoidant behaviors, further exacerbating issues.

Furthermore, a lack of preparation can hinder personal growth within the relationship. When individuals haven't taken the time to address their own needs, aspirations, and boundaries, it becomes challenging to foster an environment of mutual support and encouragement. This can lead to a stagnation of personal development, inhibiting the potential for both partners to thrive and flourish together. In addition, unaddressed insecurities or low self-esteem can contribute to feelings of inadequacy or unworthiness within the relationship. This may lead to a reliance on the partner for validation and a skewed power dynamic. Such dependencies can breed codependency and strain the overall health of the relationship.

Ultimately, the lack of preparation on an individual level can impede the overall health and sustainability of the relationship. It can lead to a cycle of unresolved issues, unmet needs, and unfulfilled expectations. Over time, this can erode the foundation of trust and mutual understanding, potentially leading to the eventual dissolution of the relationship. Therefore, taking the time for self-work, self-awareness, and personal growth before entering a relationship is not only essential for the individual's well-being but also for the health and success of the relationship as a whole. Moreover, the pursuit of personal growth leads to an increased sense of self-worth and confidence. As individuals invest in their own development, they cultivate a genuine belief in their own capabilities and worthiness of love and respect.

The Transformative Journey

As we embark on this transformative journey, it begins with self-awareness and honest reflection. It means acknowledging where we stand and whether we're truly prepared to take the next steps. It's perfectly okay to say, "I'm not ready," for God values and cherishes genuine obedience and honesty from His children. He unfailingly provides when the time is right, for His timing is always perfect. In our lives, we've often made decisions and taken actions based on our own schedules and desires. Why not truly try God?

The poignant story of Boaz and Ruth beautifully illustrates this principle. Ruth's period of waiting alongside her Mother-in-Law Naomi showcases patience, loyalty, and an unwavering work ethic. Her steadfast commitment to supporting Naomi exemplifies resilience and devotion even in her own vulnerability. Through her actions, Ruth teaches us that preparing for a new chapter often demands perseverance and a willingness to embrace humble beginnings, setting an inspiring example for each of us in our own seasons of anticipation and transition.

Chapter Activity:

Reflect on what you can do differently to prepare for your future.

Develop a plan outlining the steps you'll take to implement this change.

1.	Clarify Your Goals: Clearly define the specific changes you want to make in your life.

2.	Create an Actionable Plan: Identify the specific steps required to achieve each goal.

3.	Real Time: Develop a realistic timeline for implementing these steps.

4.	Execute and Evaluate: Regularly evaluate your progress, adjusting your approach as needed.

Notes

Chapter Three

Getting What You Desire

A Woman's Point of View

"Delight yourself in the Lord, and he will give you the desires of your heart." Psalm 37:4

Do you have a desire? Perhaps it's a new job, a home, a healthy relationship, or even the prospect of marriage. To desire something is to possess a fervent longing to attain it. However, even with a strong desire, there is still a crucial step that cannot be overlooked - preparation.

Consider the scenario of desiring a new home. It's not as simple as making the final purchase. There's a series of preparatory steps that come before that pivotal moment. Beyond securing the necessary loan, the prospective owner must also ensure that they are financially equipped to meet the demands and upkeep of their new home. Goals need to be set, plans need to be made, and readiness must be established for this newfound blessing.

Obtaining the things we desire is not the end of the journey; rather, it marks the beginning. We must be prepared to maintain and nurture our blessings, anticipating and addressing any potential obstacles that may arise. In this moment, we must ask ourselves, "Are we truly ready?"

Aligning Desires with God's Will

Desiring something and being prepared for it are two distinct states of mind when it comes to our goals and aspirations. Desire is a powerful emotional state, a fervent wish, a craving, a longing for a particular outcome, object, or experience. It can be influenced by personal preferences, societal norms, or external pressures. However, it may not always align with our current circumstances or capabilities. It is important to understand that desire alone does not guarantee success or the ability to achieve what we long for. It is primarily a mental and emotional state.

On the other hand, being ready signifies that we have the necessary skills, knowledge, resources, and preparedness to handle or attain what we desire. It encompasses a state of readiness or suitability for a particular goal or situation. Being prepared often demands prior planning, education, training, or personal development to ensure we are adequately equipped to face the challenges and responsibilities associated with our desired outcome. It is a proactive state that involves taking steps to align our capabilities with our desires, thereby increasing the likelihood of success.

Addressing Fears and Staying on the Right Path

Fear has a peculiar way of diverting us from the path that God has laid out for us. It has the potential to paralyze us, making us question our desires and hesitate in our preparations. It's imperative to confront these fears head-on, acknowledging them and seeking the strength to overcome them. By doing so, we can realign ourselves with the path that God has set for us, ensuring that our true heart's desires are in harmony with His will for our lives.

In this chapter, we will delve deeper into the process of aligning our desires with God's will. We will explore the importance of not only desiring but also being prepared for the blessings we seek. We will uncover the steps necessary to bridge the gap between desire and readiness through personal anecdotes and practical advice. As we embark on this journey, may we find the courage to confront our fears and the wisdom to discern the path that God has set before us.

Desire is a profound and multifaceted human emotion that wields significant influence over our actions and decisions, particularly in the realm of relationships and marriage. It compelled me to embark on a deep introspection, seeking to understand the true essence of desire and how it shapes our choices.

Authentic desire encompasses a fervent, genuine, and often impassioned yearning for something or someone. It fosters a profound emotional and psychological connection to a specific goal, object, or individual. This form of desire acts as a formidable driving force. It not only imbues us with vigor but also propels us into action, compelling us to surmount obstacles and confront challenges.

The sway of desire over our decision-making process is undeniable. When a desire takes root within us, it becomes a focus factor in our choices. We naturally gravitate towards actions that align with our deepest longings, guiding us along a path that leads us closer to our aspirations. Moreover, genuine desire instills a willingness to step out of our comfort zones and take calculated risks. This inclination can manifest in pursuits like career endeavors, entrepreneurial ventures, or the vulnerable act of expressing romantic interest.

In the context of marriage, desire undergoes a transformation into a profound commitment. While initial infatuation and attraction serve as crucial building blocks, enduring relationships, and marriages necessitate an abiding hunger for emotional intimacy, companionship, and shared growth. Nevertheless, desire alone cannot sustain a marriage indefinitely. With time, couples may encounter trials, and the fervor of desire may subside. A flourishing marriage calls for concerted effort in nurturing and rekindling desire through open communication, genuine intimacy, and shared life experiences.

It is paramount to acknowledge that God's design for marriage often diverges from our personal desires. His blueprint for marital union is rooted in His omniscient understanding of our needs rather than our fleeting wants. To navigate this path, we must be receptive and willing to heed His guidance. His plan is flawless, while our own aspirations may be tainted by past experiences, earthly desires, and unwise decisions. Surrendering our lives to His divine design, even in matters of the heart, requires a readiness to submit. Are we prepared to accept His chosen partner for us? Are we equipped to embark on the necessary self-improvement journey? Are we poised to be transparent and vulnerable with this individual? Are we prepared to love with a selfless, agape love? These are the essential considerations that pave the way for cherishing the divine gift bestowed upon us in the form of our future spouse.

In the grand tapestry of achieving our desires, preparation stands as a cornerstone, steering us towards a successful realization and a deeply gratifying journey.

Indeed, preparation stands as a crucial stride toward realizing our deepest desires. It lays a powerful foundation for success, offering clarity in goals, honing skills, managing resources, and fostering self-assurance. Furthermore, it paves the way for a triumphant outcome by diminishing uncertainty, amplifying efficiency, and refining decision-making. In addition, preparation promises a gratifying journey marked by personal evolution, alignment with cherished values, and a genuine appreciation for the entire process. Thus, as a widow, embracing the journey took preparation. We realized the importance of self-reflection and awareness, which were vital cornerstones of our journey to finding love once more.

Preparing for marriage is a profound and purposeful voyage that demands the concerted efforts of both partners. To embark on this enduring commitment, we each embark on a journey of self-discovery and personal advancement. Before our paths intersected, we took the time to reflect on our individual values and aspirations. When the time came for us to meet, our preparation journey prepared us to have open communication about our expectations and priorities in the relationship. Nurturing the bedrock of trust, mutual respect, and effective dialogue became paramount. It all began with meticulous preparation. Ultimately, preparing for marriage transcends the realm of wedding planning; it encompasses the cultivation of emotional and practical skills crucial for navigating the highs and lows of married life. This journey calls for unwavering dedication, patience, preparation, and the mutual envisioning of a love-filled and harmonious union.

Our past experiences, personal desires, and sometimes unwise decisions wield profound influence over our perceptions of relationships and marriage. The wounds from past betrayals or toxic dynamics can give rise to trust issues and insecurity, impeding our capacity to invest wholeheartedly in our partners. Personal desires and societal pressures may set unrealistic benchmarks, setting the stage for disillusionment when reality doesn't align with these ideals. Lingering patterns of ineffective communication, rooted in prior relationships, can hinder meaningful dialogue with our spouses. Unresolved traumas or bouts of low self-esteem may incite emotional reactions that repeat themselves in the marriage. Ultimately, our past experiences and choices, whether positive or negative, serve as the lenses through which we interpret our relationships, profoundly influencing how we navigate the intricate terrain of love and matrimony.

Preparing for a thriving marriage is an ongoing journey that demands dedication, patience, and a mutual commitment to personal and collective growth. With the loss of our first spouses, we couldn't imagine life without them or the thought of remarrying. However, we knew we had to begin the work of preparing for our next chapter. This journey of preparation for some can lead to marriage, and for others, it may not. What's important is to begin the process, start the journey, and trust God along the way. Adequate preparation, whether for marriage or other aspirations, plays an important role in achieving successful outcomes. It grants us the advantage of foresight, minimizing the uncertainties that may otherwise impede our progress. By taking the time to prepare, we gain a measure of control over our path, reducing the likelihood of being derailed by unforeseen challenges.

In my own journey as a single woman, preparation proved to be instrumental in making informed choices, particularly in the realm of dating. Over time, I became keenly aware of what I desired in my future marriage, and this clarity guided my actions.

When I encountered individuals who didn't align with what I was specifically preparing, praying, and waiting for from God, I knew not to invest unnecessary time. This readiness empowered me to make sound decisions not only in matters of the heart but also in crucial life and financial choices. Recognizing the need to shed unnecessary debt, I embarked on a deliberate financial planning journey, paying off my car and closing out my credit cards. My mindset shifted from marriage to preparing for marriage by taking care of my personal debt.

The process of desiring and pursuing a new job, home, or relationship shares foundational similarities with the quest for a healthy, fulfilling marriage. Clearly defined goals and expectations provide for a sense of fulfillment, while progress and achievements along the way bring forth joy and contentment. Just as one outlines their career objectives or envisions their dream home, those seeking marriage should articulate their values and what they seek in their future spouse. As a single mother aspiring towards marriage and diligently preparing for it, I reveled in the journey, cherishing the learning, growth, and experiences it brought. Additionally, I understood and appreciated the vital roles of patience and persistence in building a solid marital foundation.

Why not invest time and effort into preparation before marriage? The journey of marriage is filled with highs, lows, obstacles, and setbacks. Patience bestows upon couples the grace to weather these storms, affording each other the necessary time and space for growth and adaptation. It entails the understanding that not every issue can be swiftly resolved and that personal evolution is a gradual process. On the other hand, persistence signifies an unwavering commitment to surmount challenges, fortifying the relationship. It means facing difficulties head-on, learning from them, and evolving together. When combined, patience and persistence forge a resilient bond capable of withstanding the trials of time.

Chapter Activity:

This self-reflection is a crucial aspect of the preparation process. If God granted you what you've been earnestly asking for, would you be prepared to receive it?

What steps can you take to prepare yourself for what you have asked God to bless you with?

Notes

Chapter Four

Commitment to His Anointing, Will, and Desires

A Man's Point of View

In the next section, we'll explore the importance of surrendering your desires to God and how embracing His will can lead you toward a fulfilling and purpose-driven courtship. Through intentional actions and a committed heart, you can step confidently into the path that God has set before you, trusting that He will establish your plans as you commit your work to Him (Proverbs 16:3).

God has intricately designed each individual, gifting them with unique talents and abilities. These gifts serve as the bedrock of God's anointing, providing a framework through which His purpose can be expressed. When individuals wholeheartedly dedicate themselves to honing and utilizing these skills for His glory, they become vessels so His plan can come to fruition. This entails not only recognizing their inherent abilities but also actively seeking ways to refine and develop them, ensuring they can be wielded effectively in God's service.

Walking in God's Anointing

The concept of God's anointing is deeply rooted in the belief that divine empowerment and favor are bestowed upon individuals to fulfill His specific purpose for their lives. It is a spiritual consecration that equips individuals with the necessary abilities, wisdom, and discernment to carry out God's intended mission. God's anointing is not contingent on natural talents alone but is often realized through a combination of existing skills and a heartfelt commitment to serving His will.

When God places His anointing on you, He uses whatever level of skill you have to fulfill His purpose and plans for your life. God is looking for our commitment. Commitment is defined as the state of being dedicated to a cause or activity. We can't expect commitment if we can't commit to anything. We can't become fearful of moving into an unfamiliar area if God has called us there. We have to be intentional and make actionable steps, and this takes commitment. Commitment to change, commitment to new habits, and commitment to operating under God's will for our lives.

Moreover, God's anointing operates hand in hand with an individual's unwavering commitment to following His guidance and will. This commitment is characterized by a deepening faith, a surrender of personal desires to His higher purpose, and a steadfast dedication to walking in obedience. As individuals align their aspirations with God's intentions, they transform into conduits for His divine plan, channeling His power and wisdom into their pursuits.

Often, God's anointing becomes most evident when individuals step into roles or opportunities that may appear beyond their natural capabilities. It is in these moments that they realize the grace and favor of God has elevated their efforts, enabling them to achieve feats that surpass human understanding. Through God's anointing, individuals are empowered to surmount challenges, inspire others, and impact the world in ways they could not have achieved alone.

In essence, God's anointing is a synergistic relationship between an individual's existing skills, their commitment to God's Will, and His divine empowerment. It is a profound partnership that allows His purpose to be fulfilled through the unique capacities of each person. Through this sacred collaboration, individuals find fulfillment and significance in knowing that they are active participants in God's grand design for their lives.

Commitment to God's Will

Commitment is a cornerstone in operating under God's Will, signifying an unwavering dedication to aligning one's actions, decisions, and life choices with His divine plan. Embracing God's Will often demands change, both in mindset and behavior. Commitment acts as the driving force behind this transformation, providing the motivation and discipline needed to adopt new habits and embrace God's desires.

When individuals devote themselves to God's Will, they acknowledge that His wisdom surpasses their own understanding. This surrender of personal agendas and a willingness to yield to His guidance clears the path for meaningful change. It entails a conscious decision to let go of preconceived notions and embrace a higher purpose. This commitment empowers individuals to navigate through the uncertainties and challenges that change inevitably brings, trusting that God's plan is ultimately for their highest good.

Committing to God's will necessitates a profound willingness to relinquish our own limited understanding and embrace higher, divine wisdom. It entails recognizing that our human perspective is inherently confined and God's plan transcends our finite comprehension. This realization calls for a deep sense of humility, a surrendering of our ego, and an acceptance that we may not always discern what is best for us.

Furthermore, commitment plays a pivotal role in adopting new habits that align with God's desires. It necessitates a deliberate and sustained effort to cultivate behaviors that reflect His values and principles. This might involve nurturing qualities like compassion, forgiveness, and selflessness or adopting practices such as regular prayer, meditation, and acts of service. The commitment to integrate these habits into daily life is a tangible demonstration of one's dedication to living in accordance with God's Will.

Commitment to God's Will also acts as an anchor during moments of adversity and uncertainty. It provides the inner strength required to persist in the face of challenges, understanding that God's plan isn't contingent on immediate gratification or readily visible outcomes. This steadfastness empowers individuals to navigate through difficulties with grace and resilience, having faith that God is orchestrating events behind the scenes to fulfill His purposes.

Fundamentally, commitment forms the bedrock of embracing change, adopting new habits, and harmonizing with God's desires. It signifies a wholehearted dedication to His will, a readiness to undergo transformation, and an unshakable confidence in His guidance. Through commitment, individuals actively engage in the collaborative process of shaping their lives alongside God, discovering inner strength, purpose, and fulfillment along the way.

In essence, conquering the fear of the unknown and venturing into unfamiliar territory is a crucial stride in wholeheartedly embracing God's calling and purpose.

Through the cultivation of trust, a shift in perspective, seeking support, and drawing strength from past experiences of God's faithfulness, individuals can step into God's plan with assurance, confident that His guidance will lead them to a place of purpose, fulfillment, and spiritual growth.

Here's a major question: Do you know what you want? We think that we do, but a lot of times, we have no idea. In knowing what you want, you have to seek what God desires for you. And for the things that line up, you move forward. For things that do not, leave them behind. Sounds simple, right? Well, it's far from it. You have to commit to God's Will in your life to even come close to finding this out. In doing this, there is a simple but harsh reality that you must face. I don't always know what is best for me. As we said in the chapter before, our desires, a lot of times are based on past experiences. These can be good, and they can be bad. Unfortunately, bad experiences, more often than not, can influence us more than good experiences.

In my past work experience, I was once told by a superior, "We should let our customers be our billboards." He meant this in a good way, of course, but he went on to say that customers are more apt to tell others more about bad experiences rather than good ones. This is because they were affected more by the bad experience than the good one. But on the flip side of this, if we can get people to tell us about their good experiences, it will carry more weight to the people they tell. This holds true for relationships as well. We hear many horror stories from people about their bad experiences with relationships because it affected them in such a major way. But if we were to walk out God's design for relationships/marriages, it could be used to show how God's design is perfect and true. In this walk, God desires us to be available. Not perfect.

Our past experiences wield a profound influence on our desires and decision-making. Positive experiences can shape our aspirations and instill confidence in specific pursuits, while negative ones may lead to caution, fear, or a desire to avoid similar situations. When striving to align our choices with God's design, it's crucial to navigate the influence of both positive and negative experiences.

Positive experiences serve as affirmations of our capabilities and talents. They inspire us to pursue goals that resonate with our deepest passions and gifts. However, it's vital not to become too attached to specific outcomes based solely on past successes. Instead, we can use these positive experiences as a foundation for seeking God's guidance, recognizing that His plan may lead in unexpected yet ultimately fulfilling directions.

On the other hand, negative experiences can be powerful teachers. They offer valuable lessons about our limitations, the impermanence of worldly achievements, and the need for humility. While these experiences may create apprehension or caution, they can also lead to a deeper reliance on God's wisdom. It's crucial not to let past failures or disappointments define future aspirations but rather to view them as stepping stones toward a more authentic, purpose-driven path.

Our desires vs God's desires

Recognizing and articulating our true desires holds profound significance in our spiritual journey. It serves as a guiding light, directing us toward a life that harmonizes with our deepest values and convictions. When we take the time for introspection to identify our authentic desires, we lay a solid foundation upon which we can construct a purposeful and meaningful life.

In the pursuit of God's desires, we play a crucial role. His wisdom surpasses our own, and His design for us is rooted in love, purpose, and ultimate fulfillment. By seeking His counsel, we open ourselves to a higher perspective, one that transcends our limited human understanding. This divine insight helps us distinguish between our surface-level wants and what truly aligns with His will.

Our desires may often be swayed by societal norms, personal biases, or fleeting emotions. They may not always lead us toward a path that brings lasting fulfillment and aligns with our higher calling. When we earnestly seek God's desires, we invite His wisdom to illuminate the way forward. This allows us to discern between our temporary wants and the deeper, enduring desires that resonate with His plan for our lives.

Moreover, embracing God's desires empowers us to transcend the allure of instant gratification or short-term gains. It encourages patience, knowing that His timing and plan are flawless. This discernment guides us towards choices that yield enduring, transformative results rather than settling for quick fixes that may not ultimately serve our highest good.

In summary, understanding and vocalizing our genuine desires, coupled with seeking alignment with God's desires, creates a seamless integration of our human aspirations with divine guidance. This leads to a life marked by purpose, fulfillment, and synchronization with God's grand design. Consequently, it enables us to journey forward with lucidity, intentionality, and a profound sense of spiritual connection.

Practical steps in Committing to God.

In this chapter, we talked a lot about Committing to God. Here are some steps that you can take to help you in your journey to Commit to God.

Immersing oneself in sacred texts and the teachings of spiritual leaders can yield valuable insights into the nature of God's Will. It provides a framework through which individuals can begin to grasp the broader, eternal perspective from which God operates and how His plan is fundamentally rooted in love, purpose, and ultimate fulfillment.

Seeking counsel from trusted spiritual mentors or advisors can also be instrumental. These individuals can offer guidance and wisdom based on their own experiences of surrendering to God's will, reinforcing the notion that there exists a profound wisdom beyond our own understanding.

Fostering this humility commences with a genuine acknowledgment of our own fallibility. It involves recognizing that our knowledge, experiences, and perceptions are inherently limited within the vast expanse of the universe. This acknowledgment paves the way for an openness to receive guidance and wisdom from a higher source.

Prayer and meditation stand as potent tools in nurturing this humility. Engaging in a regular practice of seeking God's guidance enables individuals to quiet the clamor of their own desires and open themselves up to a higher wisdom. Through this practice, individuals can cultivate a deeper trust in God's plan, even when it may appear enigmatic or beyond immediate comprehension.

Ultimately, developing the humility to acknowledge that we don't always discern what's best for us necessitates a profound inner transformation, a willingness to relinquish control, and a deep trust in a higher power. It is a process of surrendering our limited perspective in favor of greater, divine wisdom that ultimately leads to a life of purpose, fulfillment, and alignment with God's grand design.

To navigate the influence of past experiences, we can engage in self-reflection and prayer. This allows for a deeper understanding of how past events have shaped our desires and decision-making patterns. Seeking God's guidance in this process helps us discern whether certain desires align with His plan or are rooted in personal attachments or fears.

Engaging in spiritual practices such as meditation, scripture study, and attending worship services can also provide clarity and insight. These practices create a space for us to connect with God's wisdom and discern His guidance more clearly.

Additionally, seeking counsel from trusted spiritual mentors or advisors can offer valuable perspectives on how to navigate the influence of past experiences. These individuals can provide guidance on discerning God's will in light of our unique life journey.

Ultimately, recognizing the impact of past experiences, both positive and negative, allows us to approach our desires and decision-making with a greater awareness of our own strengths, limitations, and the need for divine guidance. By seeking God's design and aligning our choices with His plan, we can move forward with a sense of purpose, trust, and confidence in the ultimate fulfillment that comes from living in accordance with His will.

In a business context, the concept of letting customers be "billboards" underscores the idea that satisfied customers can become powerful advocates for a product or service. Similarly, in relationships, this concept metaphorically highlights the significance of positive relationship experiences as a testament to the effectiveness of God's design for marriage and partnerships.

When individuals experience a healthy and thriving relationship, it stands as a tangible testament to the potential and power of God's design for human connection. A partnership characterized by love, respect, mutual support, and shared values serves as a shining example of what is achievable when two individuals align their lives in accordance with God's plan for marriage.

Much like satisfied customers eagerly sharing their positive experiences with a product or service, couples in a harmonious relationship can inspire others through their example. They become living witnesses to the transformative impact of living by God's principles. Their interactions, communication, and mutual respect serve as a testament to the beauty and effectiveness of God's design for human relationships.

Moreover, a healthy partnership can have a ripple effect on the broader community. It can serve as a wellspring of inspiration, offering hope and encouragement to those who may be facing challenges in their own relationships. It demonstrates that building a strong foundation of love and support is achievable when both partners are committed to living out God's design for marriage.

Positive relationship experiences also illuminate the intrinsic value of marriage and partnerships in God's blueprint for human flourishing. They showcase that when individuals come together in a union grounded in love and faith, they possess the potential to attain a level of fulfillment, growth, and mutual support that can be profoundly transformative.

Allowing positive relationship experiences to serve as a testimony to the effectiveness of God's design for marriage and partnerships underscores the profound impact that living in accordance with His principles can have on human relationships. It emphasizes the potential for love, growth, and mutual support that emerges when individuals align their lives with God's plan for union and companionship. Through their example, couples in thriving relationships become influential advocates for the beauty and effectiveness of God's design for human connection.

By adhering to these principles and components, couples can actively live out God's intended design for relationships and marriages. This paves the way for a partnership characterized by love, mutual respect, growth, and a profound connection to God's purpose for their union.

Understanding the distinction between being available and striving for perfection is paramount in nurturing healthy and authentic connections within relationships. Being available involves showing up emotionally and physically for one's partner, actively listening, and being present in moments of both joy and sorrow. It signifies a willingness to engage and support without expecting flawless responses or reactions. On the other hand, pursuing perfection can lead to an unrealistic quest for flawlessness, often resulting in a lack of vulnerability and an inability to acknowledge one's imperfections or shortcomings.

Embracing imperfection serves as a cornerstone for cultivating genuine and meaningful connections. When individuals are open about their vulnerabilities and imperfections, it creates an environment of trust and acceptance.

This openness allows partners to be authentic and real with each other, leading to a deeper understanding and appreciation for one another. Moreover, embracing imperfection fosters a culture of forgiveness, understanding, and mutual support. It grants the freedom to make mistakes and learn from them, promoting growth both individually and as a couple.

Ultimately, this acceptance of imperfection lays the foundation for a genuine, enduring bond founded on love, trust, and the shared journey of navigating life's highs and lows together.

.

Chapter Activity:

By recognizing and addressing these obstacles, you can take important steps toward aligning your actions with God's design for your relationship or marriage. This process of introspection and willingness to take action can lead to a deeper, more fulfilling connection with both your spouse and God's purpose for your union.

What is God waiting for you to commit to doing?
Take a moment to acknowledge any potential barriers or hesitations that may be hindering your commitment.

Notes

Chapter Five

Celebrating Your Healing Journey

A Woman's Point of View

God is not in the business of letting us down or disappointing us. He gives us space and time to learn and grow. The question is, how much time have we wasted? How much time has passed, and we have not produced the right fruit in our life?

In John 15:5, Jesus uses a powerful analogy to convey a profound spiritual truth. He compares himself to a vine and his followers to branches. This teaching emphasizes the intimate connection between believers and Christ. Just as branches draw their life, sustenance, and vitality from the vine, so do we as Christians in order to remain closely connected to Jesus to experience spiritual growth and bear the fruits of righteousness. It underscores the idea that apart from this spiritual union with Christ, our efforts and endeavors lack true meaning and effectiveness. To "bear much fruit" means to live a life aligned with God's will, characterized by love, good works, and spiritual abundance. Thus, this verse encourages believers to maintain a steadfast connection with Christ, recognizing that our spiritual life and purpose flow from this relationship. With this in mind, we should be producing fruit if we remain connected.

Fruit Inspector

A fruit inspector is an individual whose primary responsibility is to assess and evaluate the quality, condition, and characteristics of fruits and vegetables. These inspectors play a crucial role in the agricultural and food industry, ensuring that the produce meets specific standards for freshness, ripeness, size, color, and overall quality.

In the Bible, particularly in the book of Galatians (Galatians 5:22-23), there's a list of qualities referred to as the "Fruit of the Spirit," which includes love, joy, peace, patience, kindness, goodness, faithfulness, gentleness, and self-control. As believers in Christ, it is believed that Jesus evaluates our lives based on these qualities, examining whether we are manifesting the characteristics of a transformed and spiritually mature individual. So, when one says "Jesus is a fruit inspector," they are emphasizing that Jesus looks at the state of our hearts and actions to determine our spiritual growth and alignment with His teachings.

As Christians, we are encouraged to examine the fruit in our lives as a vital aspect of our spiritual journey. This self-reflection involves assessing whether we are exhibiting the qualities and virtues associated with the "Fruit of the Spirit" as outlined in the Bible. By examining our actions, attitudes, and intentions, Christians can gauge progress in becoming more Christ-like. This introspection not only helps us identify areas for improvement but also fosters personal growth, accountability, and a deeper connection with our faith. It's a practice that encourages believers to continually strive for a life that reflects the love, kindness, patience, and other virtues exemplified by Jesus, ultimately drawing closer to our spiritual goals and a closer relationship with God.

Examining our Fruit

Examining the fruit in our lives is a critical practice for Christians when preparing for marriage because it aligns with the biblical principle of living a life that honors God and reflects His love. Marriage is a sacred covenant in Christianity, and it requires a strong foundation of faith, trust, and selflessness. By evaluating our own character, values, and the "Fruit of the Spirit," we can better understand our capacity to love, forgive, and serve our future spouse in a Christ-centered marriage. This self-examination allows us to identify areas that may need improvement, fostering personal growth and spiritual maturity. Moreover, by assessing our readiness to embody qualities like patience, kindness, and faithfulness, we can enter into marriage with a clear understanding of how we can contribute positively to our relationship and create a strong, God-honoring union.

Are you bearing good fruit?

How can we say we're ready for our spouse, but we're not bearing any fruit? We have to do some self-inspection and examine the fruit in our lives. When I realized I wasn't producing healthy fruit, I had to start making some changes. I became my own fruit inspector.

As Christians, we also have to be mindful to acknowledge the fruit in our lives and witness the remarkable journey of growth and change that unfolds through our faith. By recognizing the presence of qualities like love, joy, peace, and self-control in our daily actions and interactions, we gain a deeper appreciation for the transformative work of God's grace. This acknowledgment is a source of encouragement and a reminder that our commitment to a Christ-centered life is bearing fruit in our character and relationships. It also serves as a motivation to continue nurturing these virtues, knowing that our journey of growth is an ongoing process, and with God's guidance, we can continuously strive to reflect the love and teachings of Jesus in our lives.

Time for change

On my journey to healing as a Christian, I began the process of facilitating growth and change. It started with setting aside time for self-reflection. I would regularly evaluate my thoughts, actions, and attitudes and honestly assess whether they align with the values and virtues outlined in the Bible. I even had to examine if they lined up with the future spouse I wanted to attract. Regularly evaluating your thoughts, actions, and attitudes in alignment with the values and virtues outlined in the Bible involves self-awareness. It entails a conscious effort to assess whether your decisions and behaviors resonate with biblical principles such as love, compassion, honesty, and humility. To ensure compatibility with a future spouse, I had to examine if my character, beliefs, and goals align with the qualities I sought in a partner, considering aspects like faith, morals, and life objectives. This process of developing time for self-reflection, personal growth, and effective communication helped to prepare me for the day I would meet my future spouse, who embodied the same qualities. First, it had to start with myself. How could I expect a spouse to have goals and good communication skills when I didn't?

Prayer is always key, and I began to engage in prayer and seek God for guidance and spiritual insight. I would ask God to reveal areas in my life where growth and change were needed. This is when studying the word of God and reflecting on relevant passages to inspire and guide my journey of change was needed.

You will need some support

As I embarked on my journey of healing and transformation, I recognized the need for support and guidance. I sought out an accountability partner and mentor who shared my values and faith. This invaluable connection provided a platform for open discussions about my goals and allowed for constructive feedback and encouragement.

Setting specific, measurable, and achievable goals related to the virtues I desired to cultivate in myself was crucial to my development. It required a candid assessment of where I stood and the establishment of realistic targets for growth in areas such as love, patience, kindness, and self-control.

Write it down

I began keeping a journal to capture the nuances of this transformative process. In its pages, I recorded my reflections, documented my progress, and even acknowledged moments of disappointment. This journal became a valuable record of my journey, serving as a source of motivation and a testament to my growth.

Servanthood

While waiting for change to manifest, I actively engaged with my local church and community. Serving and fellowshipping with fellow believers allowed me to put my spiritual growth and areas of development into practice. It was through these interactions that both myself and others began to witness positive changes in my life.

Acknowledging wrongs and making amends became a pivotal part of my transformation. There were moments when I had to embrace the practice of forgiveness, extending grace to both myself and those who had wronged me. This commitment to lifelong learning and spiritual growth underscored the importance of recognizing our own imperfections and seeking reconciliation.

Understanding that growth and change are processes that take time was paramount. I had to be patient with myself, celebrate achievements along the way, and trust in God's timing, even when it seemed like progress was slow. I held onto the assurance that He was continually working in my life, even in moments of apparent stagnation.

Through this journey, I began to see the fruits of my labor. Love, kindness, and humility were becoming more evident in my character. These virtues were not only a reflection of my inner transformation but also a preparation for the spouse I hoped to one day share my life with.

Chapter Activity:

Take a moment to reflect on your own healing and transformational journey. Name some specific moments of celebration, no matter how small or significant, that stand out to you. Recognize and acknowledge the progress you have made thus far.

Notes

Chapter 6

Understanding God's Purpose and Timing

A Man's Point of View

In the blueprint of life, the words we choose to utter profoundly impact our experiences, relationships, and understanding of faith and purpose. Proverbs 18:21 tells us that "The power of death and life is in the tongue," serving as a powerful reminder of the significance of our words in shaping our journey.

The Journey of Dating

Dating is a journey filled with ups, downs, and countless lessons. It's not merely about finding the right partner but also about discovering more about ourselves. In this chapter, we will explore how our words can shape our dating experiences and shed light on why seeking God's guidance is essential.

One remarkable aspect to consider is how our words can either breathe life into a budding romance or cast shadows of doubt and uncertainty. Words of affirmation, kindness, and encouragement can work wonders in building trust and creating an environment where love can truly flourish. By using our words to show appreciation and affection, we set the stage for something beautiful to develop. I experienced this transformation firsthand in my own dating journey before finding my wife. When I began using words of encouragement and affirmation, it not only brought DeAnna and myself closer but also highlighted the incredible power our words possess. We have the ability to uplift or tear down, and the choice is ours.

Conversely, negative words spoken in moments of frustration or anger can inflict lasting wounds. In the dating world, these words can lead to misunderstandings, heartache, and fractured trust. This is where the preparation stage comes into play. I realized the importance of getting myself ready for a healthy relationship. If I could speak life into my situation, imagine the impact my words would have when God eventually brought my future spouse into my life.

We've all made dating blunders, uttering words in the heat of the moment that we later regret. It is during these moments that we truly comprehend the significance of guarding our tongues. Negative words not only harm our current relationships but also shape how we approach future connections. Phrases like "There are no good men/women out there" or "I hate dating" possess more power than we realize. If we believe our words hold power, we must be vigilant about what we say.

Our Spiritual Journey

In our spiritual journey, our words hold just as much importance. Seeking God means approaching Him with an open and humble heart. Our words serve as a reflection of our heart's condition, either drawing us closer to God or creating distance. In my pursuit of understanding why seeking God is crucial, I've learned that prayer and meditation are means of communicating with Him. However, it's not just about the words themselves; it's the sincerity and intention behind them. When we approach God with genuine reverence, we invite His presence into our lives.

Positive confession is a concept worth mentioning. It revolves around speaking words of faith and positivity to manifest our desired reality. This principle applies not only to dating but to every aspect of our lives. Personally, I've found solace in praying for guidance and speaking words of trust in God's plan for my life. This practice has been transformative.

Remember, the words we speak hold immense power – they can build bridges or create barriers, uplift hearts, or cause pain. Therefore, let us choose our words with intention, speaking life, love, and faith into every aspect of our lives. As we move forward, may we continue seeking God's purpose, embracing the transformative potential of our words, and nurturing healthy, loving relationships. May this journey of faith and love be filled with blessings, growth, and an unwavering trust in God's plan for each of us. Thank you for being part of this meaningful journey. May your path ahead be illuminated with God's grace and love.

We will continue our journey of love and seek God's purpose; let us remember Proverbs 18:21. Our words have the incredible power to shape our dating experiences, relationships, and every facet of our lives. Let us choose our words wisely, speaking life, love, and faith into everything we do. By doing so, we will uncover the purpose God has for us. As we conclude this chapter and near the end of our journey, take a moment to reflect on the profound influence of our words and their impact on our dating experiences and spiritual path. It has been a journey of self-discovery, growth, and learning, and I hope you've found inspiration in the lessons we've shared.

Lesson 1 Reflection and Prayer:

Spend dedicated time in reflection and prayer. Create a space to connect with your inner thoughts and emotions and seek guidance from God.

Lesson 2 Study Scripture:

Reading and studying the Bible can provide insights into God's character, His promises, and the principles that govern His timing and purpose.

Lesson 3 Practice Patience:

Understanding God's timing often involves practicing patience. Remember that God's timing is not always aligned with our expectations, and patience is a virtue in the journey of faith.

Lesson 4 Trust in God's Sovereignty:

Encourage a deep trust in God's sovereignty. Understanding that God is in control and has a purpose for every season of life can bring comfort and peace, even in challenging times.

Lesson 5 Serve Others:

Engaging in acts of kindness and service to others can provide a sense of purpose and fulfillment. Sometimes, God's purpose is revealed through the positive impact we have on the lives of others.

Lesson 6 Connect with a Faith Community:

Being part of a faith community can offer support, encouragement, and a sense of belonging. Sharing experiences and insights with others who share similar beliefs can be enriching.

Lesson 7 Accept God's Will:

Understanding God's purpose and timing may also involve accepting that His plan might differ from personal desires. We have to have a mindset of surrender and acceptance of God's will.

Lesson 8 Keep a Spiritual Journal:

Suggest keeping a spiritual journal to document thoughts, prayers, and reflections on your journey. This can be a valuable resource for looking back and recognizing the ways God has been present in our lives.

Notes

Conclusion

The end of the beginning...

From Our Point of View

From our perspective, our love story is a testament to the power of faith, healing, and the importance of building a solid foundation for a thriving marriage. It's a story that wouldn't have unfolded as it did without our willingness to go through the process, take the necessary steps, and embrace God's plan for our relationship. Here are some of the major takeaways from this process.

The Journey of Discovery

Our journey began with self-discovery. We both recognized the importance of understanding who we truly were as individuals before embarking on a new chapter as a married couple. We dug deep, uncovered our hidden treasures, and learned to shine them brightly. Self-awareness was key to understanding how we could complement and support each other in our marriage.

Walking with God

Throughout our relationship, we've come to realize that our marriage isn't just "ours." It's God's gift to us, entrusted to our care. Our role is to nurture, provide for, and protect it, just as we would any precious gift from God. This perspective has become the cornerstone of our marriage, guiding our decisions and actions.

Embracing Imperfection

We've learned that perfection is not a requirement for a successful marriage. We have our good days and our challenging days, just like any other couple. What sets us apart is our commitment to following God's design for marriage, even when it's difficult. This means choosing to prioritize our relationship, no matter the circumstances, and being willing to die to ourselves when necessary.

Preparation Matters

Before we came together as a couple, we took the time to prepare ourselves for each other. If we had rushed into a relationship without this preparation, we might not have been able to build the strong foundation our marriage stands upon today. It was a process of self-improvement and growth, driven by our desire to honor God's plan for our union.

Healing as a Prerequisite

Healing played a vital role in our journey. Whether it's healing from the loss of a loved one, past relationships, or situations, addressing our emotional wounds was essential. We recognized that carrying baggage from previous relationships would only derail our newfound love. Healing was the key to unlocking the potential of our marriage.

Our story is a testament to the beauty that can arise when two individuals commit to nurturing a relationship under God's guidance. It's not always easy, and we're far from perfect, but our dedication to following God's design for marriage has allowed us to grow and thrive as a couple.

We share this chapter of our journey with you not as a prescription for your own path but as an inspiration to trust in the process, to prioritize healing, and to build a foundation rooted in faith and love. Your story, like ours, is unique, but it can be equally beautiful when you choose to follow God's design and nurture the precious gift of marriage He has entrusted to your care. As we reach the final pages of this book, it's important to remember that this isn't the end; it's just the beginning. The purpose of this book was to provide you with tools and experiences to help you navigate the challenging journey of loss. But let us make one thing clear: this book is merely the first step in what will be a lifetime of steps.

The most valuable advice we can offer you, the reader, is to take those first steps. In fact, take several first steps. This book has laid out a series of steps to guide you through the process, but the most significant step of all is the commitment to taking those steps. Undoubtedly, the journey itself can be filled with pain, fear, hurt, and confusion. Yet, it's also meant to be rewarding, helpful, enlightening, and empowering. The process itself is the purpose. It's designed not only to help heal you but also to allow you the opportunity to grow into the person that God has envisioned you to be, even in the midst of tragedy.

So, as you close this book, remember that the journey doesn't end here. It continues with each step you take, each moment you choose to embrace the process and each opportunity you seize to grow and heal. Your story is still unfolding, and you have the strength within you to shape it into something beautiful, even in the face of loss. This is not the end; it's just the beginning of your remarkable journey of healing, growth, and love.